Welcome

Date	Name(s)	Physical/Email Address	Telephone No.	Special Request
				☐ Contact me ☐ Pray for me ☐ Other: _____
				☐ Contact me ☐ Pray for me ☐ Other: _____
				☐ Contact me ☐ Pray for me ☐ Other: _____
				☐ Contact me ☐ Pray for me ☐ Other: _____

" There is neither Jew nor Greek, there is neither slave nor free, there is no male and female, for you are all one in Christ Jesus."
Galatians 3:28

Welcome

Date	Name(s)	Physical/Email Address	Telephone No.	Special Request
				☐ Contact me ☐ Pray for me ☐ Other: _____
				☐ Contact me ☐ Pray for me ☐ Other: _____
				☐ Contact me ☐ Pray for me ☐ Other: _____
				☐ Contact me ☐ Pray for me ☐ Other: _____

"There is neither Jew nor Greek, there is neither slave nor free, there is no male and female, for you are all one in Christ Jesus."
Galatians 3:28

Welcome

Date	Name(s)	Physical/Email Address	Telephone No.	Special Request
				☐ Contact me ☐ Pray for me ☐ Other: _____
				☐ Contact me ☐ Pray for me ☐ Other: _____
				☐ Contact me ☐ Pray for me ☐ Other: _____
				☐ Contact me ☐ Pray for me ☐ Other: _____

"There is neither Jew nor Greek, there is neither slave nor free, there is no male and female, for you are all one in Christ Jesus."
Galatians 3:28

Welcome

Date	Name(s)	Physical/Email Address	Telephone No.	Special Request
				☐ Contact me ☐ Pray for me ☐ Other: _____
				☐ Contact me ☐ Pray for me ☐ Other: _____
				☐ Contact me ☐ Pray for me ☐ Other: _____
				☐ Contact me ☐ Pray for me ☐ Other: _____

" There is neither Jew nor Greek, there is neither slave nor free, there is no male and female, for you are all one in Christ Jesus."
Galatians 3:28

Welcome

Date	Name(s)	Physical/Email Address	Telephone No.	Special Request
				☐ Contact me ☐ Pray for me ☐ Other: _____
				☐ Contact me ☐ Pray for me ☐ Other: _____
				☐ Contact me ☐ Pray for me ☐ Other: _____
				☐ Contact me ☐ Pray for me ☐ Other: _____

" There is neither Jew nor Greek, there is neither slave nor free, there is no male and female, for you are all one in Christ Jesus."
Galatians 3:28

Welcome

Date	Name(s)	Physical/Email Address	Telephone No.	Special Request
				☐ Contact me ☐ Pray for me ☐ Other: _____
				☐ Contact me ☐ Pray for me ☐ Other: _____
				☐ Contact me ☐ Pray for me ☐ Other: _____
				☐ Contact me ☐ Pray for me ☐ Other: _____

"There is neither Jew nor Greek, there is neither slave nor free, there is no male and female, for you are all one in Christ Jesus."
Galatians 3:28

Welcome

Date	Name(s)	Physical/Email Address	Telephone No.	Special Request
				☐ Contact me ☐ Pray for me ☐ Other: _____
				☐ Contact me ☐ Pray for me ☐ Other: _____
				☐ Contact me ☐ Pray for me ☐ Other: _____
				☐ Contact me ☐ Pray for me ☐ Other: _____

"There is neither Jew nor Greek, there is neither slave nor free, there is no male and female, for you are all one in Christ Jesus."
Galatians 3:28

Welcome

Date	Name(s)	Physical/Email Address	Telephone No.	Special Request
				☐ Contact me ☐ Pray for me ☐ Other: _____
				☐ Contact me ☐ Pray for me ☐ Other: _____
				☐ Contact me ☐ Pray for me ☐ Other: _____
				☐ Contact me ☐ Pray for me ☐ Other: _____

"There is neither Jew nor Greek, there is neither slave nor free, there is no male and female, for you are all one in Christ Jesus."
Galatians 3:28

Welcome

Date	Name(s)	Physical/Email Address	Telephone No.	Special Request
				☐ Contact me ☐ Pray for me ☐ Other: _____
				☐ Contact me ☐ Pray for me ☐ Other: _____
				☐ Contact me ☐ Pray for me ☐ Other: _____
				☐ Contact me ☐ Pray for me ☐ Other: _____

"There is neither Jew nor Greek, there is neither slave nor free, there is no male and female, for you are all one in Christ Jesus."
Galatians 3:28

Welcome

Date	Name(s)	Physical/Email Address	Telephone No.	Special Request
				☐ Contact me ☐ Pray for me ☐ Other: _____
				☐ Contact me ☐ Pray for me ☐ Other: _____
				☐ Contact me ☐ Pray for me ☐ Other: _____
				☐ Contact me ☐ Pray for me ☐ Other: _____

"There is neither Jew nor Greek, there is neither slave nor free, there is no male and female, for you are all one in Christ Jesus."
Galatians 3:28

Welcome

Date	Name(s)	Physical/Email Address	Telephone No.	Special Request
				☐Contact me ☐Pray for me ☐Other: _____
				☐Contact me ☐Pray for me ☐Other: _____
				☐Contact me ☐Pray for me ☐Other: _____
				☐Contact me ☐Pray for me ☐Other: _____

"There is neither Jew nor Greek, there is neither slave nor free, there is no male and female, for you are all one in Christ Jesus."
Galatians 3:28

Welcome

Date	Name(s)	Physical/Email Address	Telephone No.	Special Request
				☐ Contact me ☐ Pray for me ☐ Other: _____
				☐ Contact me ☐ Pray for me ☐ Other: _____
				☐ Contact me ☐ Pray for me ☐ Other: _____
				☐ Contact me ☐ Pray for me ☐ Other: _____

"There is neither Jew nor Greek, there is neither slave nor free, there is no male and female, for you are all one in Christ Jesus."
Galatians 3:28

Welcome

Date	Name(s)	Physical/Email Address	Telephone No.	Special Request
				☐ Contact me ☐ Pray for me ☐ Other: _____
				☐ Contact me ☐ Pray for me ☐ Other: _____
				☐ Contact me ☐ Pray for me ☐ Other: _____
				☐ Contact me ☐ Pray for me ☐ Other: _____

" There is neither Jew nor Greek, there is neither slave nor free, there is no male and female, for you are all one in Christ Jesus. "
Galatians 3:28

Welcome

Date	Name(s)	Physical/Email Address	Telephone No.	Special Request
				☐ Contact me ☐ Pray for me ☐ Other: _____
				☐ Contact me ☐ Pray for me ☐ Other: _____
				☐ Contact me ☐ Pray for me ☐ Other: _____
				☐ Contact me ☐ Pray for me ☐ Other: _____

"There is neither Jew nor Greek, there is neither slave nor free, there is no male and female, for you are all one in Christ Jesus."
Galatians 3:28

Welcome

Date	Name(s)	Physical/Email Address	Telephone No.	Special Request
				☐Contact me ☐Pray for me ☐Other: _____ _____
				☐Contact me ☐Pray for me ☐Other: _____ _____
				☐Contact me ☐Pray for me ☐Other: _____ _____
				☐Contact me ☐Pray for me ☐Other: _____ _____

"There is neither Jew nor Greek, there is neither slave nor free, there is no male and female, for you are all one in Christ Jesus."
Galatians 3:28

Welcome

Date	Name(s)	Physical/Email Address	Telephone No.	Special Request
				☐Contact me ☐Pray for me ☐Other: _____
				☐Contact me ☐Pray for me ☐Other: _____
				☐Contact me ☐Pray for me ☐Other: _____
				☐Contact me ☐Pray for me ☐Other: _____

" There is neither Jew nor Greek, there is neither slave nor free, there is no male and female, for you are all one in Christ Jesus."
Galatians 3:28

Welcome

Date	Name(s)	Physical/Email Address	Telephone No.	Special Request
				☐ Contact me ☐ Pray for me ☐ Other: _____
				☐ Contact me ☐ Pray for me ☐ Other: _____
				☐ Contact me ☐ Pray for me ☐ Other: _____
				☐ Contact me ☐ Pray for me ☐ Other: _____

"There is neither Jew nor Greek, there is neither slave nor free, there is no male and female, for you are all one in Christ Jesus."
Galatians 3:28

Date	Name(s)	Physical/Email Address	Telephone No.	Special Request
				☐ Contact me ☐ Pray for me ☐ Other: _____
				☐ Contact me ☐ Pray for me ☐ Other: _____
				☐ Contact me ☐ Pray for me ☐ Other: _____
				☐ Contact me ☐ Pray for me ☐ Other: _____

"There is neither Jew nor Greek, there is neither slave nor free, there is no male and female, for you are all one in Christ Jesus."
Galatians 3:28

Welcome

Date	Name(s)	Physical/Email Address	Telephone No.	Special Request
				☐ Contact me ☐ Pray for me ☐ Other: _____ _____
				☐ Contact me ☐ Pray for me ☐ Other: _____ _____
				☐ Contact me ☐ Pray for me ☐ Other: _____ _____
				☐ Contact me ☐ Pray for me ☐ Other: _____ _____

"There is neither Jew nor Greek, there is neither slave nor free, there is no male and female, for you are all one in Christ Jesus."
Galatians 3:28

Welcome

Date	Name(s)	Physical/Email Address	Telephone No.	Special Request
				☐ Contact me ☐ Pray for me ☐ Other: _____
				☐ Contact me ☐ Pray for me ☐ Other: _____
				☐ Contact me ☐ Pray for me ☐ Other: _____
				☐ Contact me ☐ Pray for me ☐ Other: _____

"There is neither Jew nor Greek, there is neither slave nor free, there is no male and female, for you are all one in Christ Jesus."
Galatians 3:28

Welcome

Date	Name(s)	Physical/Email Address	Telephone No.	Special Request
				☐ Contact me ☐ Pray for me ☐ Other: _____
				☐ Contact me ☐ Pray for me ☐ Other: _____
				☐ Contact me ☐ Pray for me ☐ Other: _____
				☐ Contact me ☐ Pray for me ☐ Other: _____

"There is neither Jew nor Greek, there is neither slave nor free, there is no male and female, for you are all one in Christ Jesus."
Galatians 3:28

Welcome

Date	Name(s)	Physical/Email Address	Telephone No.	Special Request
				☐ Contact me ☐ Pray for me ☐ Other: _____
				☐ Contact me ☐ Pray for me ☐ Other: _____
				☐ Contact me ☐ Pray for me ☐ Other: _____
				☐ Contact me ☐ Pray for me ☐ Other: _____

"There is neither Jew nor Greek, there is neither slave nor free, there is no male and female, for you are all one in Christ Jesus."
Galatians 3:28

Welcome

Date	Name(s)	Physical/Email Address	Telephone No.	Special Request
				☐Contact me ☐Pray for me ☐Other: _____
				☐Contact me ☐Pray for me ☐Other: _____
				☐Contact me ☐Pray for me ☐Other: _____
				☐Contact me ☐Pray for me ☐Other: _____

"There is neither Jew nor Greek, there is neither slave nor free, there is no male and female, for you are all one in Christ Jesus."
Galatians 3:28

Welcome

Date	Name(s)	Physical/Email Address	Telephone No.	Special Request
				☐ Contact me ☐ Pray for me ☐ Other: _____
				☐ Contact me ☐ Pray for me ☐ Other: _____
				☐ Contact me ☐ Pray for me ☐ Other: _____
				☐ Contact me ☐ Pray for me ☐ Other: _____

"There is neither Jew nor Greek, there is neither slave nor free, there is no male and female, for you are all one in Christ Jesus."
Galatians 3:28

Welcome

Date	Name(s)	Physical/Email Address	Telephone No.	Special Request
				☐ Contact me ☐ Pray for me ☐ Other: _____
				☐ Contact me ☐ Pray for me ☐ Other: _____
				☐ Contact me ☐ Pray for me ☐ Other: _____
				☐ Contact me ☐ Pray for me ☐ Other: _____

"There is neither Jew nor Greek, there is neither slave nor free, there is no male and female, for you are all one in Christ Jesus."
Galatians 3:28

Welcome

Date	Name(s)	Physical/Email Address	Telephone No.	Special Request
				☐ Contact me ☐ Pray for me ☐ Other: _____
				☐ Contact me ☐ Pray for me ☐ Other: _____
				☐ Contact me ☐ Pray for me ☐ Other: _____
				☐ Contact me ☐ Pray for me ☐ Other: _____

"There is neither Jew nor Greek, there is neither slave nor free, there is no male and female, for you are all one in Christ Jesus."
Galatians 3:28

Welcome

Date	Name(s)	Physical/Email Address	Telephone No.	Special Request
				☐Contact me ☐Pray for me ☐Other: _____
				☐Contact me ☐Pray for me ☐Other: _____
				☐Contact me ☐Pray for me ☐Other: _____
				☐Contact me ☐Pray for me ☐Other: _____

"There is neither Jew nor Greek, there is neither slave nor free, there is no male and female, for you are all one in Christ Jesus."
Galatians 3:28

Welcome

Date	Name(s)	Physical/Email Address	Telephone No.	Special Request
				☐ Contact me ☐ Pray for me ☐ Other: _____
				☐ Contact me ☐ Pray for me ☐ Other: _____
				☐ Contact me ☐ Pray for me ☐ Other: _____
				☐ Contact me ☐ Pray for me ☐ Other: _____

"There is neither Jew nor Greek, there is neither slave nor free, there is no male and female, for you are all one in Christ Jesus."
Galatians 3:28

Welcome

Date	Name(s)	Physical/Email Address	Telephone No.	Special Request
				☐ Contact me ☐ Pray for me ☐ Other: _____
				☐ Contact me ☐ Pray for me ☐ Other: _____
				☐ Contact me ☐ Pray for me ☐ Other: _____
				☐ Contact me ☐ Pray for me ☐ Other: _____

"There is neither Jew nor Greek, there is neither slave nor free, there is no male and female, for you are all one in Christ Jesus."
Galatians 3:28

Welcome

Date	Name(s)	Physical/Email Address	Telephone No.	Special Request
				☐ Contact me ☐ Pray for me ☐ Other: _____
				☐ Contact me ☐ Pray for me ☐ Other: _____
				☐ Contact me ☐ Pray for me ☐ Other: _____
				☐ Contact me ☐ Pray for me ☐ Other: _____

"There is neither Jew nor Greek, there is neither slave nor free, there is no male and female, for you are all one in Christ Jesus."
Galatians 3:28

Welcome

Date	Name(s)	Physical/Email Address	Telephone No.	Special Request
				☐Contact me ☐Pray for me ☐Other: _____
				☐Contact me ☐Pray for me ☐Other: _____
				☐Contact me ☐Pray for me ☐Other: _____
				☐Contact me ☐Pray for me ☐Other: _____

"There is neither Jew nor Greek, there is neither slave nor free, there is no male and female, for you are all one in Christ Jesus."
Galatians 3:28

Welcome

Date	Name(s)	Physical/Email Address	Telephone No.	Special Request
				☐ Contact me ☐ Pray for me ☐ Other: _____
				☐ Contact me ☐ Pray for me ☐ Other: _____
				☐ Contact me ☐ Pray for me ☐ Other: _____
				☐ Contact me ☐ Pray for me ☐ Other: _____

"There is neither Jew nor Greek, there is neither slave nor free, there is no male and female, for you are all one in Christ Jesus."
Galatians 3:28

Welcome

Date	Name(s)	Physical/Email Address	Telephone No.	Special Request
				☐ Contact me ☐ Pray for me ☐ Other: _____
				☐ Contact me ☐ Pray for me ☐ Other: _____
				☐ Contact me ☐ Pray for me ☐ Other: _____
				☐ Contact me ☐ Pray for me ☐ Other: _____

"There is neither Jew nor Greek, there is neither slave nor free, there is no male and female, for you are all one in Christ Jesus."
Galatians 3:28

Welcome

Date	Name(s)	Physical/Email Address	Telephone No.	Special Request
				☐ Contact me ☐ Pray for me ☐ Other: _____
				☐ Contact me ☐ Pray for me ☐ Other: _____
				☐ Contact me ☐ Pray for me ☐ Other: _____
				☐ Contact me ☐ Pray for me ☐ Other: _____

"There is neither Jew nor Greek, there is neither slave nor free, there is no male and female, for you are all one in Christ Jesus."
Galatians 3:28

Welcome

Date	Name(s)	Physical/Email Address	Telephone No.	Special Request
				☐Contact me ☐Pray for me ☐Other: _____
				☐Contact me ☐Pray for me ☐Other: _____
				☐Contact me ☐Pray for me ☐Other: _____
				☐Contact me ☐Pray for me ☐Other: _____

"There is neither Jew nor Greek, there is neither slave nor free, there is no male and female, for you are all one in Christ Jesus."
Galatians 3:28

Welcome

Date	Name(s)	Physical/Email Address	Telephone No.	Special Request
				☐ Contact me ☐ Pray for me ☐ Other: _____
				☐ Contact me ☐ Pray for me ☐ Other: _____
				☐ Contact me ☐ Pray for me ☐ Other: _____
				☐ Contact me ☐ Pray for me ☐ Other: _____

"There is neither Jew nor Greek, there is neither slave nor free, there is no male and female, for you are all one in Christ Jesus."
Galatians 3:28

Welcome

Date	Name(s)	Physical/Email Address	Telephone No.	Special Request
				☐ Contact me ☐ Pray for me ☐ Other: _____
				☐ Contact me ☐ Pray for me ☐ Other: _____
				☐ Contact me ☐ Pray for me ☐ Other: _____
				☐ Contact me ☐ Pray for me ☐ Other: _____

" There is neither Jew nor Greek, there is neither slave nor free, there is no male and female, for you are all one in Christ Jesus."
Galatians 3:28

Welcome

Date	Name(s)	Physical/Email Address	Telephone No.	Special Request
				☐ Contact me ☐ Pray for me ☐ Other: _____
				☐ Contact me ☐ Pray for me ☐ Other: _____
				☐ Contact me ☐ Pray for me ☐ Other: _____
				☐ Contact me ☐ Pray for me ☐ Other: _____

"There is neither Jew nor Greek, there is neither slave nor free, there is no male and female, for you are all one in Christ Jesus."
Galatians 3:28

Welcome

Date	Name(s)	Physical/Email Address	Telephone No.	Special Request
				☐Contact me ☐Pray for me ☐Other: _____
				☐Contact me ☐Pray for me ☐Other: _____
				☐Contact me ☐Pray for me ☐Other: _____
				☐Contact me ☐Pray for me ☐Other: _____

"There is neither Jew nor Greek, there is neither slave nor free, there is no male and female, for you are all one in Christ Jesus."
Galatians 3:28

Welcome

Date	Name(s)	Physical/Email Address	Telephone No.	Special Request
				☐Contact me ☐Pray for me ☐Other: _____
				☐Contact me ☐Pray for me ☐Other: _____
				☐Contact me ☐Pray for me ☐Other: _____
				☐Contact me ☐Pray for me ☐Other: _____

"There is neither Jew nor Greek, there is neither slave nor free, there is no male and female, for you are all one in Christ Jesus."
Galatians 3:28

Welcome

Date	Name(s)	Physical/Email Address	Telephone No.	Special Request
				☐ Contact me ☐ Pray for me ☐ Other: _____
				☐ Contact me ☐ Pray for me ☐ Other: _____
				☐ Contact me ☐ Pray for me ☐ Other: _____
				☐ Contact me ☐ Pray for me ☐ Other: _____

"There is neither Jew nor Greek, there is neither slave nor free, there is no male and female, for you are all one in Christ Jesus."
Galatians 3:28

Welcome

Date	Name(s)	Physical/Email Address	Telephone No.	Special Request
				☐Contact me ☐Pray for me ☐Other: _____
				☐Contact me ☐Pray for me ☐Other: _____
				☐Contact me ☐Pray for me ☐Other: _____
				☐Contact me ☐Pray for me ☐Other: _____

"There is neither Jew nor Greek, there is neither slave nor free, there is no male and female, for you are all one in Christ Jesus."
Galatians 3:28

Welcome

Date	Name(s)	Physical/Email Address	Telephone No.	Special Request
				☐Contact me ☐Pray for me ☐Other: _____
				☐Contact me ☐Pray for me ☐Other: _____
				☐Contact me ☐Pray for me ☐Other: _____
				☐Contact me ☐Pray for me ☐Other: _____

"There is neither Jew nor Greek, there is neither slave nor free, there is no male and female, for you are all one in Christ Jesus."
Galatians 3:28

Welcome

Date	Name(s)	Physical/Email Address	Telephone No.	Special Request
				☐ Contact me ☐ Pray for me ☐ Other: _____
				☐ Contact me ☐ Pray for me ☐ Other: _____
				☐ Contact me ☐ Pray for me ☐ Other: _____
				☐ Contact me ☐ Pray for me ☐ Other: _____

"There is neither Jew nor Greek, there is neither slave nor free, there is no male and female, for you are all one in Christ Jesus."
Galatians 3:28

Welcome

Date	Name(s)	Physical/Email Address	Telephone No.	Special Request
				☐ Contact me ☐ Pray for me ☐ Other: _____
				☐ Contact me ☐ Pray for me ☐ Other: _____
				☐ Contact me ☐ Pray for me ☐ Other: _____
				☐ Contact me ☐ Pray for me ☐ Other: _____

" There is neither Jew nor Greek, there is neither slave nor free, there is no male and female, for you are all one in Christ Jesus."
Galatians 3:28

Welcome

Date	Name(s)	Physical/Email Address	Telephone No.	Special Request
				☐ Contact me ☐ Pray for me ☐ Other: _____
				☐ Contact me ☐ Pray for me ☐ Other: _____
				☐ Contact me ☐ Pray for me ☐ Other: _____
				☐ Contact me ☐ Pray for me ☐ Other: _____

"There is neither Jew nor Greek, there is neither slave nor free, there is no male and female, for you are all one in Christ Jesus."
Galatians 3:28

Welcome

Date	Name(s)	Physical/Email Address	Telephone No.	Special Request
				☐Contact me ☐Pray for me ☐Other: _____
				☐Contact me ☐Pray for me ☐Other: _____
				☐Contact me ☐Pray for me ☐Other: _____
				☐Contact me ☐Pray for me ☐Other: _____

"There is neither Jew nor Greek, there is neither slave nor free, there is no male and female, for you are all one in Christ Jesus."
Galatians 3:28

Welcome

Date	Name(s)	Physical/Email Address	Telephone No.	Special Request
				☐ Contact me ☐ Pray for me ☐ Other: _____ _____
				☐ Contact me ☐ Pray for me ☐ Other: _____ _____
				☐ Contact me ☐ Pray for me ☐ Other: _____ _____
				☐ Contact me ☐ Pray for me ☐ Other: _____ _____

" There is neither Jew nor Greek, there is neither slave nor free, there is no male and female, for you are all one in Christ Jesus."
Galatians 3:28

Welcome

Date	Name(s)	Physical/Email Address	Telephone No.	Special Request
				☐Contact me ☐Pray for me ☐Other: _____ _____
				☐Contact me ☐Pray for me ☐Other: _____ _____
				☐Contact me ☐Pray for me ☐Other: _____ _____
				☐Contact me ☐Pray for me ☐Other: _____ _____

"There is neither Jew nor Greek, there is neither slave nor free, there is no male and female, for you are all one in Christ Jesus."
Galatians 3:28

Welcome

Date	Name(s)	Physical/Email Address	Telephone No.	Special Request
				☐Contact me ☐Pray for me ☐Other: _____
				☐Contact me ☐Pray for me ☐Other: _____
				☐Contact me ☐Pray for me ☐Other: _____
				☐Contact me ☐Pray for me ☐Other: _____

"There is neither Jew nor Greek, there is neither slave nor free, there is no male and female, for you are all one in Christ Jesus."
Galatians 3:28

Welcome

Date	Name(s)	Physical/Email Address	Telephone No.	Special Request
				☐Contact me ☐Pray for me ☐Other: _____
				☐Contact me ☐Pray for me ☐Other: _____
				☐Contact me ☐Pray for me ☐Other: _____
				☐Contact me ☐Pray for me ☐Other: _____

"There is neither Jew nor Greek, there is neither slave nor free, there is no male and female, for you are all one in Christ Jesus."
Galatians 3:28

Welcome

Date	Name(s)	Physical/Email Address	Telephone No.	Special Request
				☐ Contact me ☐ Pray for me ☐ Other: _____
				☐ Contact me ☐ Pray for me ☐ Other: _____
				☐ Contact me ☐ Pray for me ☐ Other: _____
				☐ Contact me ☐ Pray for me ☐ Other: _____

"There is neither Jew nor Greek, there is neither slave nor free, there is no male and female, for you are all one in Christ Jesus."
Galatians 3:28

Welcome

Date	Name(s)	Physical/Email Address	Telephone No.	Special Request
				☐ Contact me ☐ Pray for me ☐ Other: _____
				☐ Contact me ☐ Pray for me ☐ Other: _____
				☐ Contact me ☐ Pray for me ☐ Other: _____
				☐ Contact me ☐ Pray for me ☐ Other: _____

"There is neither Jew nor Greek, there is neither slave nor free, there is no male and female, for you are all one in Christ Jesus."
Galatians 3:28

Date	Name(s)	Physical/Email Address	Telephone No.	Special Request
				☐ Contact me ☐ Pray for me ☐ Other: _____
				☐ Contact me ☐ Pray for me ☐ Other: _____
				☐ Contact me ☐ Pray for me ☐ Other: _____
				☐ Contact me ☐ Pray for me ☐ Other: _____

"There is neither Jew nor Greek, there is neither slave nor free, there is no male and female, for you are all one in Christ Jesus."
Galatians 3:28

Welcome

Date	Name(s)	Physical/Email Address	Telephone No.	Special Request
				☐ Contact me ☐ Pray for me ☐ Other: _____
				☐ Contact me ☐ Pray for me ☐ Other: _____
				☐ Contact me ☐ Pray for me ☐ Other: _____
				☐ Contact me ☐ Pray for me ☐ Other: _____

"There is neither Jew nor Greek, there is neither slave nor free, there is no male and female, for you are all one in Christ Jesus."
Galatians 3:28

Welcome

Date	Name(s)	Physical/Email Address	Telephone No.	Special Request
				☐ Contact me ☐ Pray for me ☐ Other: _____
				☐ Contact me ☐ Pray for me ☐ Other: _____
				☐ Contact me ☐ Pray for me ☐ Other: _____
				☐ Contact me ☐ Pray for me ☐ Other: _____

"There is neither Jew nor Greek, there is neither slave nor free, there is no male and female, for you are all one in Christ Jesus."
Galatians 3:28

Welcome

Date	Name(s)	Physical/Email Address	Telephone No.	Special Request
				☐ Contact me ☐ Pray for me ☐ Other: _____
				☐ Contact me ☐ Pray for me ☐ Other: _____
				☐ Contact me ☐ Pray for me ☐ Other: _____
				☐ Contact me ☐ Pray for me ☐ Other: _____

"There is neither Jew nor Greek, there is neither slave nor free, there is no male and female, for you are all one in Christ Jesus."
Galatians 3:28

Welcome

Date	Name(s)	Physical/Email Address	Telephone No.	Special Request
				☐ Contact me ☐ Pray for me ☐ Other: _____
				☐ Contact me ☐ Pray for me ☐ Other: _____
				☐ Contact me ☐ Pray for me ☐ Other: _____
				☐ Contact me ☐ Pray for me ☐ Other: _____

"There is neither Jew nor Greek, there is neither slave nor free, there is no male and female, for you are all one in Christ Jesus."
Galatians 3:28

Welcome

Date	Name(s)	Physical/Email Address	Telephone No.	Special Request
				☐ Contact me ☐ Pray for me ☐ Other: _____
				☐ Contact me ☐ Pray for me ☐ Other: _____
				☐ Contact me ☐ Pray for me ☐ Other: _____
				☐ Contact me ☐ Pray for me ☐ Other: _____

"There is neither Jew nor Greek, there is neither slave nor free, there is no male and female, for you are all one in Christ Jesus."
Galatians 3:28

Welcome

Date	Name(s)	Physical/Email Address	Telephone No.	Special Request
				☐Contact me ☐Pray for me ☐Other: _____
				☐Contact me ☐Pray for me ☐Other: _____
				☐Contact me ☐Pray for me ☐Other: _____
				☐Contact me ☐Pray for me ☐Other: _____

"There is neither Jew nor Greek, there is neither slave nor free, there is no male and female, for you are all one in Christ Jesus."
Galatians 3:28

Welcome

Date	Name(s)	Physical/Email Address	Telephone No.	Special Request
				☐ Contact me ☐ Pray for me ☐ Other: _____
				☐ Contact me ☐ Pray for me ☐ Other: _____
				☐ Contact me ☐ Pray for me ☐ Other: _____
				☐ Contact me ☐ Pray for me ☐ Other: _____

"There is neither Jew nor Greek, there is neither slave nor free, there is no male and female, for you are all one in Christ Jesus."
Galatians 3:28

Welcome

Date	Name(s)	Physical/Email Address	Telephone No.	Special Request
				☐ Contact me ☐ Pray for me ☐ Other: _____ _____
				☐ Contact me ☐ Pray for me ☐ Other: _____ _____
				☐ Contact me ☐ Pray for me ☐ Other: _____ _____
				☐ Contact me ☐ Pray for me ☐ Other: _____ _____

"There is neither Jew nor Greek, there is neither slave nor free, there is no male and female, for you are all one in Christ Jesus."
Galatians 3:28

Welcome

Date	Name(s)	Physical/Email Address	Telephone No.	Special Request
				☐ Contact me ☐ Pray for me ☐ Other: _____ _____
				☐ Contact me ☐ Pray for me ☐ Other: _____ _____
				☐ Contact me ☐ Pray for me ☐ Other: _____ _____
				☐ Contact me ☐ Pray for me ☐ Other: _____ _____

" There is neither Jew nor Greek, there is neither slave nor free, there is no male and female, for you are all one in Christ Jesus."
Galatians 3:28

Welcome

Date	Name(s)	Physical/Email Address	Telephone No.	Special Request
				☐Contact me ☐Pray for me ☐Other: _____ _____
				☐Contact me ☐Pray for me ☐Other: _____ _____
				☐Contact me ☐Pray for me ☐Other: _____ _____
				☐Contact me ☐Pray for me ☐Other: _____ _____

"There is neither Jew nor Greek, there is neither slave nor free, there is no male and female, for you are all one in Christ Jesus."
Galatians 3:28

Welcome

Date	Name(s)	Physical/Email Address	Telephone No.	Special Request
				☐Contact me ☐Pray for me ☐Other: _____
				☐Contact me ☐Pray for me ☐Other: _____
				☐Contact me ☐Pray for me ☐Other: _____
				☐Contact me ☐Pray for me ☐Other: _____

"There is neither Jew nor Greek, there is neither slave nor free, there is no male and female, for you are all one in Christ Jesus."
Galatians 3:28

Welcome

Date	Name(s)	Physical/Email Address	Telephone No.	Special Request
				☐ Contact me ☐ Pray for me ☐ Other: _____
				☐ Contact me ☐ Pray for me ☐ Other: _____
				☐ Contact me ☐ Pray for me ☐ Other: _____
				☐ Contact me ☐ Pray for me ☐ Other: _____

"There is neither Jew nor Greek, there is neither slave nor free, there is no male and female, for you are all one in Christ Jesus."
Galatians 3:28

Welcome

Date	Name(s)	Physical/Email Address	Telephone No.	Special Request
				☐Contact me ☐Pray for me ☐Other: _____
				☐Contact me ☐Pray for me ☐Other: _____
				☐Contact me ☐Pray for me ☐Other: _____
				☐Contact me ☐Pray for me ☐Other: _____

"There is neither Jew nor Greek, there is neither slave nor free, there is no male and female, for you are all one in Christ Jesus."
Galatians 3:28

Welcome

Date	Name(s)	Physical/Email Address	Telephone No.	Special Request
				☐ Contact me ☐ Pray for me ☐ Other: _____
				☐ Contact me ☐ Pray for me ☐ Other: _____
				☐ Contact me ☐ Pray for me ☐ Other: _____
				☐ Contact me ☐ Pray for me ☐ Other: _____

"There is neither Jew nor Greek, there is neither slave nor free, there is no male and female, for you are all one in Christ Jesus."
Galatians 3:28

Welcome

Date	Name(s)	Physical/Email Address	Telephone No.	Special Request
				☐ Contact me ☐ Pray for me ☐ Other: _____
				☐ Contact me ☐ Pray for me ☐ Other: _____
				☐ Contact me ☐ Pray for me ☐ Other: _____
				☐ Contact me ☐ Pray for me ☐ Other: _____

" There is neither Jew nor Greek, there is neither slave nor free, there is no male and female, for you are all one in Christ Jesus."
Galatians 3:28

Welcome

Date	Name(s)	Physical/Email Address	Telephone No.	Special Request
				☐ Contact me ☐ Pray for me ☐ Other: _____ _____
				☐ Contact me ☐ Pray for me ☐ Other: _____ _____
				☐ Contact me ☐ Pray for me ☐ Other: _____ _____
				☐ Contact me ☐ Pray for me ☐ Other: _____ _____

"There is neither Jew nor Greek, there is neither slave nor free, there is no male and female, for you are all one in Christ Jesus."
Galatians 3:28

Welcome

Date	Name(s)	Physical/Email Address	Telephone No.	Special Request
				☐ Contact me ☐ Pray for me ☐ Other: _____
				☐ Contact me ☐ Pray for me ☐ Other: _____
				☐ Contact me ☐ Pray for me ☐ Other: _____
				☐ Contact me ☐ Pray for me ☐ Other: _____

"There is neither Jew nor Greek, there is neither slave nor free, there is no male and female, for you are all one in Christ Jesus."
Galatians 3:28

Welcome

Date	Name(s)	Physical/Email Address	Telephone No.	Special Request
				☐ Contact me ☐ Pray for me ☐ Other: _____
				☐ Contact me ☐ Pray for me ☐ Other: _____
				☐ Contact me ☐ Pray for me ☐ Other: _____
				☐ Contact me ☐ Pray for me ☐ Other: _____

"There is neither Jew nor Greek, there is neither slave nor free, there is no male and female, for you are all one in Christ Jesus."
Galatians 3:28

Welcome

Date	Name(s)	Physical/Email Address	Telephone No.	Special Request
				☐ Contact me ☐ Pray for me ☐ Other: _____
				☐ Contact me ☐ Pray for me ☐ Other: _____
				☐ Contact me ☐ Pray for me ☐ Other: _____
				☐ Contact me ☐ Pray for me ☐ Other: _____

"There is neither Jew nor Greek, there is neither slave nor free, there is no male and female, for you are all one in Christ Jesus."
Galatians 3:28

Welcome

Date	Name(s)	Physical/Email Address	Telephone No.	Special Request
				☐ Contact me ☐ Pray for me ☐ Other: _____
				☐ Contact me ☐ Pray for me ☐ Other: _____
				☐ Contact me ☐ Pray for me ☐ Other: _____
				☐ Contact me ☐ Pray for me ☐ Other: _____

"There is neither Jew nor Greek, there is neither slave nor free, there is no male and female, for you are all one in Christ Jesus."
Galatians 3:28

Welcome

Date	Name(s)	Physical/Email Address	Telephone No.	Special Request
				☐ Contact me ☐ Pray for me ☐ Other: _____
				☐ Contact me ☐ Pray for me ☐ Other: _____
				☐ Contact me ☐ Pray for me ☐ Other: _____
				☐ Contact me ☐ Pray for me ☐ Other: _____

" There is neither Jew nor Greek, there is neither slave nor free, there is no male and female, for you are all one in Christ Jesus."
Galatians 3:28

Welcome

Date	Name(s)	Physical/Email Address	Telephone No.	Special Request
				☐ Contact me ☐ Pray for me ☐ Other: _____
				☐ Contact me ☐ Pray for me ☐ Other: _____
				☐ Contact me ☐ Pray for me ☐ Other: _____
				☐ Contact me ☐ Pray for me ☐ Other: _____

"There is neither Jew nor Greek, there is neither slave nor free, there is no male and female, for you are all one in Christ Jesus."
Galatians 3:28

Welcome

Date	Name(s)	Physical/Email Address	Telephone No.	Special Request
				☐ Contact me ☐ Pray for me ☐ Other: _____
				☐ Contact me ☐ Pray for me ☐ Other: _____
				☐ Contact me ☐ Pray for me ☐ Other: _____
				☐ Contact me ☐ Pray for me ☐ Other: _____

"There is neither Jew nor Greek, there is neither slave nor free, there is no male and female, for you are all one in Christ Jesus."
Galatians 3:28

Welcome

Date	Name(s)	Physical/Email Address	Telephone No.	Special Request
				☐Contact me ☐Pray for me ☐Other: _____
				☐Contact me ☐Pray for me ☐Other: _____
				☐Contact me ☐Pray for me ☐Other: _____
				☐Contact me ☐Pray for me ☐Other: _____

"There is neither Jew nor Greek, there is neither slave nor free, there is no male and female, for you are all one in Christ Jesus."
Galatians 3:28

Welcome

Date	Name(s)	Physical/Email Address	Telephone No.	Special Request
				☐ Contact me ☐ Pray for me ☐ Other: _____
				☐ Contact me ☐ Pray for me ☐ Other: _____
				☐ Contact me ☐ Pray for me ☐ Other: _____
				☐ Contact me ☐ Pray for me ☐ Other: _____

" There is neither Jew nor Greek, there is neither slave nor free, there is no male and female, for you are all one in Christ Jesus."
Galatians 3:28

Welcome

Date	Name(s)	Physical/Email Address	Telephone No.	Special Request
				☐ Contact me ☐ Pray for me ☐ Other: _____
				☐ Contact me ☐ Pray for me ☐ Other: _____
				☐ Contact me ☐ Pray for me ☐ Other: _____
				☐ Contact me ☐ Pray for me ☐ Other: _____

"There is neither Jew nor Greek, there is neither slave nor free, there is no male and female, for you are all one in Christ Jesus."
Galatians 3:28

Welcome

Date	Name(s)	Physical/Email Address	Telephone No.	Special Request
				☐ Contact me ☐ Pray for me ☐ Other: _____ _____
				☐ Contact me ☐ Pray for me ☐ Other: _____ _____
				☐ Contact me ☐ Pray for me ☐ Other: _____ _____
				☐ Contact me ☐ Pray for me ☐ Other: _____ _____

" There is neither Jew nor Greek, there is neither slave nor free, there is no male and female, for you are all one in Christ Jesus."
Galatians 3:28

Welcome

Date	Name(s)	Physical/Email Address	Telephone No.	Special Request
				☐Contact me ☐Pray for me ☐Other: _____
				☐Contact me ☐Pray for me ☐Other: _____
				☐Contact me ☐Pray for me ☐Other: _____
				☐Contact me ☐Pray for me ☐Other: _____

"There is neither Jew nor Greek, there is neither slave nor free, there is no male and female, for you are all one in Christ Jesus."
Galatians 3:28

Welcome

Date	Name(s)	Physical/Email Address	Telephone No.	Special Request
				☐ Contact me ☐ Pray for me ☐ Other: _____
				☐ Contact me ☐ Pray for me ☐ Other: _____
				☐ Contact me ☐ Pray for me ☐ Other: _____
				☐ Contact me ☐ Pray for me ☐ Other: _____

"There is neither Jew nor Greek, there is neither slave nor free, there is no male and female, for you are all one in Christ Jesus."
Galatians 3:28

Welcome

Date	Name(s)	Physical/Email Address	Telephone No.	Special Request
				☐ Contact me ☐ Pray for me ☐ Other: _____ _____
				☐ Contact me ☐ Pray for me ☐ Other: _____ _____
				☐ Contact me ☐ Pray for me ☐ Other: _____ _____
				☐ Contact me ☐ Pray for me ☐ Other: _____ _____

"There is neither Jew nor Greek, there is neither slave nor free, there is no male and female, for you are all one in Christ Jesus."
Galatians 3.28

Welcome

Date	Name(s)	Physical/Email Address	Telephone No.	Special Request
				☐Contact me ☐Pray for me ☐Other: _____
				☐Contact me ☐Pray for me ☐Other: _____
				☐Contact me ☐Pray for me ☐Other: _____
				☐Contact me ☐Pray for me ☐Other: _____

"There is neither Jew nor Greek, there is neither slave nor free, there is no male and female, for you are all one in Christ Jesus."
Galatians 3:28

Welcome

Date	Name(s)	Physical/Email Address	Telephone No.	Special Request
				☐ Contact me ☐ Pray for me ☐ Other: _____
				☐ Contact me ☐ Pray for me ☐ Other: _____
				☐ Contact me ☐ Pray for me ☐ Other: _____
				☐ Contact me ☐ Pray for me ☐ Other: _____

"There is neither Jew nor Greek, there is neither slave nor free, there is no male and female, for you are all one in Christ Jesus."
Galatians 3:28

Welcome

Date	Name(s)	Physical/Email Address	Telephone No.	Special Request
				☐ Contact me ☐ Pray for me ☐ Other: _____
				☐ Contact me ☐ Pray for me ☐ Other: _____
				☐ Contact me ☐ Pray for me ☐ Other: _____
				☐ Contact me ☐ Pray for me ☐ Other: _____

"There is neither Jew nor Greek, there is neither slave nor free, there is no male and female, for you are all one in Christ Jesus."
Galatians 3:28

Welcome

Date	Name(s)	Physical/Email Address	Telephone No.	Special Request
				☐ Contact me ☐ Pray for me ☐ Other: _____
				☐ Contact me ☐ Pray for me ☐ Other: _____
				☐ Contact me ☐ Pray for me ☐ Other: _____
				☐ Contact me ☐ Pray for me ☐ Other: _____

"There is neither Jew nor Greek, there is neither slave nor free, there is no male and female, for you are all one in Christ Jesus."
Galatians 3:28

Welcome

Date	Name(s)	Physical/Email Address	Telephone No.	Special Request
				☐ Contact me ☐ Pray for me ☐ Other: _____ _____
				☐ Contact me ☐ Pray for me ☐ Other: _____ _____
				☐ Contact me ☐ Pray for me ☐ Other: _____ _____
				☐ Contact me ☐ Pray for me ☐ Other: _____ _____

"There is neither Jew nor Greek, there is neither slave nor free, there is no male and female, for you are all one in Christ Jesus."
Galatians 3:28

Welcome

Date	Name(s)	Physical/Email Address	Telephone No.	Special Request
				☐ Contact me ☐ Pray for me ☐ Other: _____
				☐ Contact me ☐ Pray for me ☐ Other: _____
				☐ Contact me ☐ Pray for me ☐ Other: _____
				☐ Contact me ☐ Pray for me ☐ Other: _____

"There is neither Jew nor Greek, there is neither slave nor free, there is no male and female, for you are all one in Christ Jesus."
Galatians 3:28

Welcome

Date	Name(s)	Physical/Email Address	Telephone No.	Special Request
				☐Contact me ☐Pray for me ☐Other: _____
				☐Contact me ☐Pray for me ☐Other: _____
				☐Contact me ☐Pray for me ☐Other: _____
				☐Contact me ☐Pray for me ☐Other: _____

"There is neither Jew nor Greek, there is neither slave nor free, there is no male and female, for you are all one in Christ Jesus."
Galatians 3:28

Welcome

Date	Name(s)	Physical/Email Address	Telephone No.	Special Request
				☐Contact me ☐Pray for me ☐Other: _____
				☐Contact me ☐Pray for me ☐Other: _____
				☐Contact me ☐Pray for me ☐Other: _____
				☐Contact me ☐Pray for me ☐Other: _____

"There is neither Jew nor Greek, there is neither slave nor free, there is no male and female, for you are all one in Christ Jesus."
Galatians 3:28

Welcome

Date	Name(s)	Physical/Email Address	Telephone No.	Special Request
				☐Contact me ☐Pray for me ☐Other: _____ _____
				☐Contact me ☐Pray for me ☐Other: _____ _____
				☐Contact me ☐Pray for me ☐Other: _____ _____
				☐Contact me ☐Pray for me ☐Other: _____ _____

"There is neither Jew nor Greek, there is neither slave nor free, there is no male and female, for you are all one in Christ Jesus."
Galatians 3:28

Welcome

Date	Name(s)	Physical/Email Address	Telephone No.	Special Request
				☐Contact me ☐Pray for me ☐Other: _____
				☐Contact me ☐Pray for me ☐Other: _____
				☐Contact me ☐Pray for me ☐Other: _____
				☐Contact me ☐Pray for me ☐Other: _____

" There is neither Jew nor Greek, there is neither slave nor free, there is no male and female, for you are all one in Christ Jesus."
Galatians 3:28

Welcome

Date	Name(s)	Physical/Email Address	Telephone No.	Special Request
				☐Contact me ☐Pray for me ☐Other: _____ _____
				☐Contact me ☐Pray for me ☐Other: _____ _____
				☐Contact me ☐Pray for me ☐Other: _____ _____
				☐Contact me ☐Pray for me ☐Other: _____ _____

"There is neither Jew nor Greek, there is neither slave nor free, there is no male and female, for you are all one in Christ Jesus."
Galatians 3:28

Welcome

Date	Name(s)	Physical/Email Address	Telephone No.	Special Request
				☐ Contact me ☐ Pray for me ☐ Other: _____
				☐ Contact me ☐ Pray for me ☐ Other: _____
				☐ Contact me ☐ Pray for me ☐ Other: _____
				☐ Contact me ☐ Pray for me ☐ Other: _____

"There is neither Jew nor Greek, there is neither slave nor free, there is no male and female, for you are all one in Christ Jesus."
Galatians 3:28

Welcome

Date	Name(s)	Physical/Email Address	Telephone No.	Special Request
				☐ Contact me ☐ Pray for me ☐ Other: _____
				☐ Contact me ☐ Pray for me ☐ Other: _____
				☐ Contact me ☐ Pray for me ☐ Other: _____
				☐ Contact me ☐ Pray for me ☐ Other: _____

"There is neither Jew nor Greek, there is neither slave nor free, there is no male and female, for you are all one in Christ Jesus."
Galatians 3:28

Welcome

Date	Name(s)	Physical/Email Address	Telephone No.	Special Request
				☐Contact me ☐Pray for me ☐Other: _____
				☐Contact me ☐Pray for me ☐Other: _____
				☐Contact me ☐Pray for me ☐Other: _____
				☐Contact me ☐Pray for me ☐Other: _____

"There is neither Jew nor Greek, there is neither slave nor free, there is no male and female, for you are all one in Christ Jesus."
Galatians 3:28

Welcome

Date	Name(s)	Physical/Email Address	Telephone No.	Special Request
				☐ Contact me ☐ Pray for me ☐ Other: _____
				☐ Contact me ☐ Pray for me ☐ Other: _____
				☐ Contact me ☐ Pray for me ☐ Other: _____
				☐ Contact me ☐ Pray for me ☐ Other: _____

" There is neither Jew nor Greek, there is neither slave nor free, there is no male and female, for you are all one in Christ Jesus."
Galatians 3:28

Welcome

Date	Name(s)	Physical/Email Address	Telephone No.	Special Request
				☐Contact me ☐Pray for me ☐Other: _____
				☐Contact me ☐Pray for me ☐Other: _____
				☐Contact me ☐Pray for me ☐Other: _____
				☐Contact me ☐Pray for me ☐Other: _____

"There is neither Jew nor Greek, there is neither slave nor free, there is no male and female, for you are all one in Christ Jesus."
Galatians 3:28